THE PEAK PERFORMANCE
MANUAL FOR YOUR MIND

GAVIN DRAKE | JOHN JACKSON

bookshaker

First Published In Great Britain 2013
by www.BookShaker.com

CONTENTS

THE MINDSPAN TRIAD

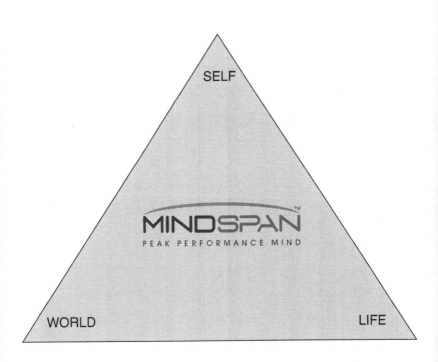

INTRODUCTION

"And you may ask yourself,
Well, how did I get here?"

"Once In A Lifetime", Talking Heads

So, just how did you get here?

Why have you decided to read this book?

People's answers to these questions will be different, but they will all have something in common. They will all, somewhere, include a desire to discover or develop new ways of doing things. These new ways will all arise from another common aim—a heartfelt desire to bring about improvement.

This is exactly what this book is designed to help you achieve.

You may also be wondering why, if they are so knowledgeable about achieving excellence in personal performance, would the people writing this book want to share this learning with anyone else? Wouldn't it be better to keep the secrets safely under lock and key and reap whatever rewards were available for themselves?

It is a good question and, as a first step towards answering, it let me recall a brief anecdote from my past.

In the mid 1990s, I experienced a number of what a friend of mine called those "Wouldn't it be great if…" moments. In my case, "Wouldn't it be great if I started my own business?" I had a good job, a nice house, a lovely wife, a growing family and an enviably secure future. But although I was happy and fulfilled, I knew there was something more I wanted. Something was missing and I wanted more from my life. In particular I wanted to make a difference to other people's lives by branching out and setting up my own business as a psychological performance specialist. I knew that I wouldn't really feel fulfilled or reach my true potential unless I took that risk.

I was, in the context of this book, my very own personal case study. At one end of the shoreline of personal decision lay the "What's the worst thing that can happen?" question and at the other the fulfilment of a genuine dream. With some personal courage, hard work and the welcome support of others, this ambition continues to unfold. By taking the necessary steps and accepting full responsibility for my actions, my life has been transformed.

It has been the success of this journey that has led me to make a further decision: to want to make available to others the knowledge and experience that I have gained and am still acquiring. The motive, if there needs to be one, is simple: I feel that I have a duty to do so.

I don't mean duty in the classical, buttoned-up, king and country sense of the word. Rather it springs from a genuine sense of personal and social responsibility. As I often say to people, "I just want to get all this stuff out there!" By far the most precious resource we have in our lives is time and if we could all use it to the best advantage, how much happier would individuals be and how much healthier the society and world in which we live?

My values were shaped when I was quite young. My mother died unexpectedly when I was twelve years old. Even though, as a naïve boy, I didn't realise the true importance of this sudden tragedy, it was without doubt a pivotal moment in my life. As a reflective and mature adult, I can see very clearly the effect it has had upon me and how this has shaped my whole approach to life.

It brought into sharp focus that each one of us faces the real possibility of experiencing personal waste and loss—unfulfilled potential. Time, our most valuable resource, is not to be treated lightly.

It is said that we have some 60,000 thoughts each day. Let this one be the starting point of this book and the motivation for what you will find in the pages ahead.

*

This book has been growing and developing for some time in a restless, embryonic fashion. I see it as a publication which I hope will enhance the lives of the people who read it.

I have spent many years engrossed in the study of human psychology. I have read innumerable books and publications of all kinds and attended a wide array of conferences and meetings. Teaching mental performance programmes has given me an enormous interest in the way that individuals think, what they think about and how they become aware of their own patterns of thought. These insights have provided the energy and motivation for my involvement in this subject area.

As a teenager I was probably an under-achiever, in truth a bit of a lost soul, lacking focus and unable to apply myself fully to anything. My early employment with a footwear company allowed me access to the world of intensive management training and a new passion for learning that has never left me. As a very young manager, I discovered the real enjoyment that can arise from developing others and I began my own journey of personal growth and development. At the heart of it all, bubbling away in my mind at that point in my life, was the huge but also simple question, "Why do we do what we do?" It might also have been the unconscious question that had haunted my life until that moment.

Everything I have done since then has led me to three important realisations; the tenets that will inform everything that follows:

1. If you want to improve any aspect of your life at any time, first look at your own psychology to see where change may need to take place. The same imperative applies to individuals in any organisation. You need first to work on people's psychology if you truly want to improve organisational results.

2. Trying to get the world to fit you all of the time is not just impossible but a complete waste of time and effort.
3. If you change the way you look at things, the things you look at will change.

In this book I have built upon what I have learnt and used over many years to raise issues, examine and re-examine other people's ideas and develop new concepts. Although these are based upon sound theoretical understanding, I want to engage your emotions as well as intellect. We will also focus on the practical application of these ideas to real-life, empirical situations in many, diverse arenas of human endeavour.

I trust that you will find it an absorbing and rewarding journey.

Gavin Drake

MindSpan
Foundations

SECTION ONE

PERFORMANCE SICKNESS, PERFORMANCE HEALTH

"Hanging on in quiet desperation is the English way"

Pink Floyd, "Time", Dark Side of the Moon

Performance Sickness

I firmly believe that, if asked, most people would say that they wanted to be as successful as they can be in their lives, whatever that might mean to them. Indeed, it's difficult to imagine why anyone wouldn't. But if a second, more specific, question were to follow, "How well do you think you are actually doing?" the answer would probably be found in one of the following four possible categories:

1. I would find it hard to do any better than I am now
2. I'm ok, but I know that I could do better
3. I'm doing as much as I need to when I need to do it
4. I'm really not achieving much at all other than just about getting by

If you, the reader, can say that you fall into any of the last three bands then I would suggest very strongly that you are probably suffering from what I describe as "Performance Sickness". This may well come as a surprise to you.

It is essential, therefore, to clarify what I mean by this. The definition of the term, Performance Sickness, that I have coined, is:

"Any mental, emotional or behavioural aspect of ourselves that drives a performance limit short of where we want to be."

This can reveal itself in a multitude of different ways with different people and in similar and contrasting organisations. Here are just a few example symptoms: ...

- Continuing friction in a valuable work or personal relationship
- Poor sales results
- Non achievement of targets
- Ineffective management or leadership
- Low quality communication
- Lack of confidence in important situations
- Putting off key activities in favour of unimportant, comfortable tasks
- Overtly aggressive behaviour
- Lack of motivation
- Low levels of commitment
- Moaning, whingeing and complaining

Like many other forms of illness, Performance Sickness can be diagnosed and treated, but a remedy can only be prescribed if you really have had enough of your condition and want to make improvements to its inverse, your Performance

Health. Also, like many other forms of poor health, Performance Sickness can lurk within you without fatal consequences but, as it does so, it will steadily sap away your energy and prevent you from achieving all you can in life.

Clearly, every one of us may underachieve for a variety of reasons, sometimes in combination, that can be traced back to our psychology, our feelings and the context in which we live and work. I take the position that in searching for reasons for underperformance our drive should always be to look into ourselves. To reach maximum potential in our lives it is essential that we take full responsibility for what we do and not rely upon or seek to blame anyone else for the results and outcomes we achieve.

Over the many years that I have been delivering training programmes and other developmental activities, I have met many thousands of people, perhaps as many as 5,000 per year. Without exception they want, as individuals, partners and parents, to be happy, satisfied and challenged people. The vast majority of these individuals are extremely hardworking, often juggling demanding careers, long hours, travel and family responsibilities.

Increasingly, as I observe and admire their tireless efforts, I wonder just what kind of return they are achieving for this major and relentless investment of energy. Business people often talk about ROI or Return On Investment, but for these individuals I wonder about their ROE, their Return On Energy.

Whilst I have made great efforts in my life to focus my own available energies in a rational and careful way on clear, overall aims and targets, I fear that many of the people I see have a very low ROE in their lives. Many seem to be completely unaware that they are suffering from Performance Sickness. They don't realise that they are "ill" and this in itself may exacerbate their failing condition.

Sadly, or perhaps, luckily, it is only when a major life event occurs—an illness, a fatality, a loss of long-held assumptions—that people stop to consider what they are really doing. We have all heard these conversations as people realise that they are often on a rather pointless and meaningless treadmill. This, without doubt, is a terrible shame and perhaps it is an indictment on us all that it takes these moments for us to find the time and wherewithal to stop and ask ourselves these vital questions.

In order to begin to identify the type or level of performance sickness that you may be suffering, here is a simple self-assessment audit. Take some time and work your way through it.

MindSpan Personal Performance Health Audit
Please read each of the following statements and score yourself using the scale provided. There are no right or wrong answers so be honest in your responses. Your honesty will help you to learn about yourself, provide valuable information and feedback that will be helpful to you and from which may arise the awareness and opportunity for new and positive action.

1 – Never   2 – Rarely   3 – Sometimes   4 – Often   5 – Consistently

1. I start the day with a positive attitude   1 2 3 4 5

2. I focus positively in situations on what I want to achieve   1 2 3 4 5

3. I perform to a high level in my work roles   1 2 3 4 5

4. I perform to a high level in my life roles   1 2 3 4 5

5. I adopt positive beliefs for myself about my capabilities   1 2 3 4 5

6. I am clear about the choices I need to make to give me

     the life I want   1 2 3 4 5

7. I take responsibility for my actions (do not blame others

     for what I do)   1 2 3 4 5

8. I praise myself when I do things well   1 2 3 4 5

9. I enjoy stepping out of my comfort zone and doing

     new things   1 2 3 4 5

10. I am a highly confident person   1 2 3 4 5

11. I comfortably give compliments to other people   1 2 3 4 5

12. I feel able to handle the challenges that life gives me   1 2 3 4 5

13. I am a happy person   1 2 3 4 5

14. I am a fulfilled person   1 2 3 4 5

15. Wherever I am physically, I make sure I am mentally

     present and concentrating   1 2 3 4 5

16. I am grateful for the time I am given daily   1 2 3 4 5

17. I treat time as precious resource that I spend wisely   1 2 3 4 5

18. I appreciate the great number of things I have in my

     life that are good   1 2 3 4 5

19. I feel calm and in control of my life and what I do   1 2 3 4 5

20. I spend time considering what I want out of life   1 2 3 4 5

21. I have real clarity about what I want to achieve in

the short, medium and long term   1 2 3 4 5

22. I have a healthy work/life balance   1 2 3 4 5

23. I set well constructed goals for myself in work   1 2 3 4 5

24. I set well constructed goals for myself in life   1 2 3 4 5

25. I regularly visualise what I want to achieve   1 2 3 4 5

26. I am proactive in changing things in my life that I want

to improve   1 2 3 4 5

27. I spend my energies wisely on things that give me the life

I want   1 2 3 4 5

28. I manage my emotional state well   1 2 3 4 5

29. I consider setbacks as an opportunity for personal growth   1 2 3 4 5

30. I deal with situations and people in a way that limits

my stress   1 2 3 4 5

31. I work hard to understand other people's views   1 2 3 4 5

32. I have strong, positive influence with people   1 2 3 4 5

33. I help people to feel valued   1 2 3 4 5

34. I am patient with people and a good listener   1 2 3 4 5

35. I am empathetic towards others   1 2 3 4 5

36. I receive lots of willing cooperation from other people   1 2 3 4 5

37. I am confident building relationships with others   1 2 3 4 5

38. I spend time learning and developing myself   1 2 3 4 5

39. I eat well and undertake activities that make me healthy   1 2 3 4 5

40. I sleep well   1 2 3 4 5

Now add up your scores for each of the 40 statements to discover your Personal Performance Health total:

Then plot yourself on the following scale:

It is worth pointing out at this stage that there is probably no-one on earth who is not experiencing some degree of Performance Sickness in their lives. For all of us there are certain areas of our lives that are not as we would like them ideally to be. These are, of course, the elements of our lives that we would particularly like to improve.

Equally, it is likely that everyone is also experiencing a level of Performance Health, enjoying certain areas of our lives exactly as we would like them to be.

It is all a matter of degree. I have met people who have very high levels of Performance Sickness in that most areas of their lives seem to be failing. I have met others who display very obvious signs of

Performance Health because most areas of their lives are vibrant, fulfilling and successful.

What I really want to help you do is to become aware of your own degrees of Performance Sickness and Health.

But also, I want you, from the very start, to fix firmly in your mind that we all have it within ourselves to be Performance Healthy to a very high level.

So I would ask you – how much do you want to live a life that for you is *really* worth living?

MINDSPAN FOUNDATIONS SECTION ONE KEY POINTS

- If you can honestly say that you are currently achieving all the outcomes in your life that you want, you are enjoying a high level of "Performance Health"

- The great majority of us, however, are probably suffering from some kind of "Performance Sickness" in that we are not as effective in some aspects of our lives and work as we know we are capable of being
- There are many common symptoms of this that are quite easy to spot if you are aware of what you are looking and listening for
- This condition manifests itself in the results and outcomes we are achieving in our everyday lives
- To gain a good understanding of exactly where you are at the moment, undertake a Personal Performance Health Audit

From the results and new level of self-awareness you gain from the audit, you can start taking action to improve what it is that's important to you.

SECTION TWO

THE IMPORTANCE OF PERSONAL THINKING

*"The spaceman says everybody look down,
It's all in your mind"*

The Killers, "Spaceman", Day and Age

You have begun to identify in some detail the degrees of performance sickness that may exist in some or even many areas of your life. You have also had the opportunity to focus in on what you would like to change to bring about improvements in your engagement with the world.

When I started working in the field of enhanced personal performance, in all kinds of public and private organisations, one thing soon became very clear to me. It was that most of the people I was working with believed very strongly that their circumstances were responsible for creating the results they were achieving in their lives. More than a decade on, I am more convinced than ever that this is not the case. I believe strongly that every result you achieve in life is in some way the product of your thinking.

As individual human beings in an increasingly complex world, we very rarely have complete control over the circumstances we find ourselves in. We perceive that we are pushed and pulled by the bigger forces around us and the relationships we find ourselves involved in.

Nevertheless, it is true to say that we all have far more control than we may believe we have over what we choose to think about, what is happening around us and, crucially, how we choose to think about it.

So let's banish this myth here and now, once and for all: circumstances don't have a stranglehold on the results that you can expect from life. It's your thinking that counts and it's your thinking that will determine where you go and what you do.

Take a look at this diagram.

It is generally agreed in the field of human psychology that this is the way that every human being functions...

RESULTS

↑

HABITS

↑

ACTIONS

↑

EMOTIONS

↑

THINKING

It is from this starting point that we will look in this chapter at two questions which follow logically from this chart:

What is it that has brought you to this point in your life?

How can you begin using this new knowledge to take the first steps towards creating a future in which you can achieve everything you really want to?

Let me start to answer these with the following observations.

The first of these is that your brain, those few pounds of matter packed inside your skull, is working 24-hours a day, seven days a week. It is a constant furnace of mental activity, functioning consciously, subconsciously—even when you are deeply asleep. While you are alive there is no point at which it isn't working. Secondly, it is generally agreed that there is a direct, causal relationship between the way we think and the way we feel. In other words, quite simply, it is our thinking that creates and drives our emotional state and in turn this affects and shapes our behaviour.

If you believe that this assertion needs to be supported by solid evidence, you can easily test it right now.

Since you've been reading this book, you may have begun to think in positive and constructive ways about it. If you thought the cover attractive, the ideas interesting and the audit in the previous chapter useful, you have become emotionally engaged with this book. As a result, you will be feeling content with your choice of reading, keen to read more and even, perhaps, interested in finding out more about the subject.

If this is the case, you may also have become aware that these feelings are beginning to drive your behaviour. You will find it easy to read on quickly with full engagement and close attention, looking forward to completing the enjoyable journey that you have just embarked upon.

Conversely, if your thinking has been different, perhaps quite the opposite, you have probably begun to notice strong signs of disengagement.

These will include a recognisable difficulty in reading on, page-skipping, maybe a desire to give up and do something else. Perhaps you are even considering sending me an email about your negative feelings.

This very simple example serves not just as proof of the assertion that thoughts drive our emotions, it is, a model that can be applied to any situation that we find ourselves in. The way we think about ourselves, our lives and the world around us, directly impacts upon and affects our emotional state; this results in a particular kind of connected or disconnected behaviour. It is a simple and easily observable formula.

So where does all this take us? Where can we identify the circumstances which could interfere with and shape our performance in a negative fashion? Let's consider the following...

Most people have heard of the "Monday morning feeling". The weekend is over, the alarm clock rings, it's warm inside the house and grey, dull and rainy outside. It's an effort to open the curtains fully. For some people, this is a mental trigger for an emotional and physical slump which is in no way conducive to performance health. If it happens every week, perhaps in a similar way every day, the individual concerned eventually wakes each morning already in a depressed, down state, even though they may not know exactly why. The conscious drip-feeding has morphed into a sub-conscious habitual state of mind. It is much like a self-fulfilling prophecy.

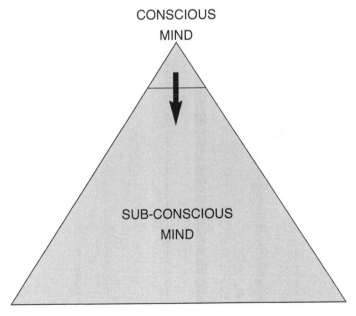

CONSCIOUS
MIND

SUB-CONSCIOUS
MIND

In this diagram, we can see how negative thoughts can bring about unhelpful, even damaging, outcomes in anybody's life.

The same can be applied to many other situations, from road rage to shouting at the television.

In starting to answer the two questions I posed at the beginning of this chapter, I would ask you to take a further step and open yourself to a more difficult question.

What is it in your thinking that is contributing to any of your own unsatisfactory states of affairs?

We will continue to look in increasing detail at this important issue; just *how* it is that our thinking brings about the satisfaction or discontent that we are experiencing in our lives.

As an initial step we need to consider carefully the relationship between the conscious and the subconscious mind. What we know is that the conscious mind is at all times drip-feeding the subconscious. That is, the thoughts we have are not just elusive, ethereal whims, but are real, physical signals passing through our brains. What the conscious mind repeats consistently the subconscious happily accepts and eventually takes off its hands, smoothly assuming control. We have all seen what happens when people start to take a new route across a lawn or through a forest. What starts as barely discernible footsteps soon becomes a trail of worn ground which in turns develops into a wide, readily visible and easily useable pathway. This is what is happening in our brains with what are called neural pathways.

On any given day, the number of our actions that result from our conscious thinking is very, very small. It has been estimated that the trillion brain cells each one of us possesses create up to 60,000 thoughts each day, but that a tiny proportion of these are generated by the metaphorical laser beam of our conscious mind. The vast majority of our mind is working on a subconscious level, dictating our behaviour in a repetitive, habitual manner.

Take the example of driving. When we take nervously to the roads in a vehicle for the first few times, everything we do is predominantly and, often, painfully conscious. In rapid and relentless succession we tell ourselves to concentrate on the clutch, the gears, the brake, the road and so on, microsecond by anxious microsecond.

However, after a period of time things ease considerably and it is likely that our one and only point of conscious attention is on the road ahead. The subconscious has begun to kick in and is guiding a large number of actions and responses that not so long ago were at the very front of our conscious minds.

So how does this come about? How can it be that some 95% of our actions are subconsciously generated: breathing, walking, chewing and the like?

To use a nautical analogy, the conscious mind is the captain of the ship and the subconscious is the crew. The subconscious crew is eager and willing to do the captain's bidding and guide the ship in a dutifully conditioned fashion. It is happy if its superior is left to do little more than admire the view from the deck above. What starts as an isolated event can become, with time, a consistent characteristic that has been generated by assimilated repetition. The crew are sailing the ship consistently into either calm seas or, perhaps, troubled waters as the captain sits in his cabin.

Despite the focus on the negative aspects of this process, we can, nonetheless, stop to ponder what incredible, phenomenal creatures we are. Our brains are strange and powerful things. It is vital to realise and remain aware that just as negative thinking can produce unhealthy results, so positive thinking can bring about an ability to undertake and complete very complex activities very safely. Just think: as well as driving most of us can swim, ride a bike or write an email with very few conscious problems. We are capable of doing so many things so very well.

So, to answer, finally, the second of the original questions, it is necessary to embrace this new level of awareness and indulge in what is called meta-cognition. This means to take the time to think about the way we think. Be honest and candid in your analysis of your own thoughts. How do you think about the situations you find yourself in? Is it possible to sit attentively on your own shoulder and gain a new perspective on the way your mind is working? Can you raise yourself up high enough to stand guard at the door of your own mind?

In the next chapter we will be taking the first steps towards this important goal.

MINDSPAN FOUNDATIONS SECTION TWO
KEY POINTS

- Every outcome that you achieve in your life can be traced back as a direct outcome of your thinking.
- All of us have more control over what we are thinking about and, most importantly, how we are thinking about it, than we realise.

- It is our thinking that shapes and drives our emotional state and this in turn determines the nature of our behaviour. Our behaviours and responses then shape our results in life.
- Negative thinking can therefore generate unhelpful emotions which will lead to even less useful forms of behaviour.
- The conscious mind drip-feeds the subconscious, creating habits of thought and approach that determine the way we see the world and our responses to it.
- It is essential therefore to become very aware of what and how we think to develop a level of meta-cognition, or thinking about our thinking, that will make this apparent and available to us.
- Our brains are complex and powerful machines and it is possible to programme them with regular, positive inputs that over time become new and successful habits.

Your Self
Psychology

SECTION ONE

YOUR BRAIN CAN'T DO A DON'T
SO STOP TRYING "NOT TO"!

*"You say it's not what you do,
It's what you're thinking of"*

The Ting Tings, "Be The One", We Started Nothing

Let me set you a challenge.

To help you gain clarity about how you are currently thinking and to begin the process of helping you to find new ways of doing so which will bring you what you want, I would like you to consider carefully the following scenario.

The challenge is this: imagine that on the floor in front of you there is a straight line, 15 metres long. If you can walk from one end of the line to the other in a perfectly straight line there will be a reward of two free tickets to a top-class show in your area. Can you do it?

Of course you can. Easily. It's a simple task for a generous reward.

In fact it's so straightforward and you are so clever that you can do it without much thought, in a calm and relaxed fashion.

Now, what if I were to set you the same challenge but change the surrounding circumstances just a little…

Imagine you are a member of a construction team perching on the very top of the steel framework of a tall skyscraper currently being built. You are standing on a steel girder 30 centimetres wide, 15 metres long—and 100 metres in the air.

One of your colleagues is standing at the other end of the girder and he is offering the same two tickets, but only if you are prepared to come and claim them.

Take a moment. Would you still take up this attractive offer? And if you did, would you still walk along the 15 metres in the same calm and relaxed fashion? Probably not.

Let's take some time to explain the differences between these two scenarios built around the same challenge. Remember that ultimately, in both cases, you are being asked to walk 15 metres along a straight line. In the normal course of things, this is a task that should not disturb or overwhelm any one of us.

When you are walking the line across the floor your focus is solely on the achievement of your goal. Compare this with your focus when you are 100 metres up in the air.

In this situation most people would be thinking only of what they don't want to happen, of not falling, of not ending their lives. But when you think about *not* falling, what you're actually thinking about is falling. You create within your mind and central nervous system the very experience of falling. It is a common and understandable mental reaction. So let's consider just how damaging this type of focus could be to your health in this situation.

If you are focusing entirely on not falling and all that this disaster would entail, maybe looking constantly down at the ground 100 metres below your feet, what will be happening to your heart rate and your breathing? Will you be perspiring uncontrollably? Will your legs turn to jelly? Or will your whole body just freeze and refuse to move?

There is little doubt that in this extreme set of circumstances, the fact you are focusing on what you do not want to happen will actually be making this unwanted result more likely to occur.

Let's look at a true story from my own working life as a real-life illustration.

I once worked with a woman who held a senior position in a large organisation. She had ambitions to be promoted or move on to a better post elsewhere. The problem was that when she took part in meetings she became very emotional and would invariably burst into tears. Quite obviously this did not put her in a strong position for whatever promotions became available.

When I helped her to delve into why this was happening we found that before these meetings she was spending virtually all her time and mental energy on efforts to help her not to cry. Unfortunately, as we have seen above, this just did not work. In fact it created its own inevitable outcome. Working with her, we turned attention away from avoiding the negative to a focus on positive behaviours. Sure enough, in her next meeting, having changed her thinking, she successfully put forward her ideas without tears in a calm, controlled and confident manner. She has since moved on to greater heights in her profession.

This simple example tells us a great deal about how the human brain works.

As I said at the start of this section, the human brain can't do a don't. It really struggles to process negatively expressed goals in a positive way.

Let's look at another everyday example: when my children were much younger, around five or six years old, they sometimes asked if they could have a glass of milk in the evening and I would tell them to help themselves from the cartons in the fridge. Their initial request was often followed by another a few minutes later. Could they, please, take their milk into the living room to watch the television?

Usually I gave them the response they were looking for, but would almost always add that they must be very careful not to spill their milk in there. It didn't happen every time, but there were lots of spillages that I remember from that period.

Now, clearly, as their father I can't control totally my children's thinking and focus, but I do have a potentially very strong influence upon these in my choice of language, attitude and behaviour. The moment I tell them in a stern voice not to spill their milk, their focus is directed straight to the possibility of this happening.

Let's take this a little further. Imagine that you are in a group of 10 people, all family and friends, celebrating a special occasion in a restaurant. You are seated around one big table enjoying a special evening of good food and pleasant company. As the time passes, pockets of happy conversation develop within the group.

If, at this point, one member of the group pipes up with, "Hey, don't look now but Brad Pitt has just walked in!" Just what do you think everyone will do?

Try it again, in a slightly different form, right now. If I tell you to try your hardest for the next few seconds not to think of an elephant… what are you thinking of?

So why should this be the case?

The reason is that the human brain works teleologically. In other words, in the way it functions it is very end- and goal-orientated. It wants to complete what it has in mind. However it doesn't differentiate between a "do" and a "don't". What your mind focuses on is what you will inevitably gravitate towards, like a heat-seeking missile locking doggedly on to its target.

There are basically three ways that human beings focus in any situation:

- Expecting to fail—knowing that it will all inevitably go very wrong
- Trying not to fail—making the very best effort not to mess things up
- Expecting to succeed—focusing on doing a good job, on what you want to happen and achieve

Over the past decade or so, I have worked with cricketers who have gone from scoring regular ducks to hitting centuries; with footballers badly out of form who have returned to the top of their game; driving test failures who have sailed through their next test;

and sales people who have regained their ability to serve their customers properly and hit their sales targets. All of this has been achieved by getting them to change their focus, moving them forward to look for and expect success.

Here's a more concrete example of how this can work, this time on a team basis:

In 2005 I was doing some work with the young trainee footballers in Norwich City's Academy. The first team had been relegated from the Premiership the previous year and were struggling to hold their own even in the much lowlier environment of the Championship. They had won just two games out of the last 11 and were in a troubling 18th place in the division. This was the situation when I received a call from the manager, Nigel Worthington, to come and run a session on thinking and focus with these under-performing players.

I was delighted to be asked and worked quickly with the team to examine, understand and change their thinking. They had slipped into a mindset somewhere between trying not to lose and expecting defeat. Their recent record showed this well. What I would like you to note here is that we spent no time working on ball skills, strategy, tactics, personal fitness or diet. What I did was to offer them some precious time and the opportunity to address and reframe their thinking from focusing on what they didn't want to what they did. The next day Norwich played Crewe Alexandra away and were one nil down at half time. Had they followed their usual habits, they would have capitulated and accepted yet another defeat. Armed with their new found belief, the second half saw them turn the game around and run out winners by two goals to one. Happily, this change of focus continued into further winning games and the downward slide was halted.

This example demonstrates very forcibly that the teleological brain drives you to gravitate towards what you focus on, good or bad, and what you focus on you make bigger and more pressing in your life. In the vast array of life's unfolding circumstances and situations, it is essential that you focus on what you want, not what you don't want.

In other words, your brain can't do a don't. So stop trying not to!

YOUR SELF PSYCHOLOGY SECTION ONE
KEY POINTS

- Each one of us has a way of focusing on the kinds of outcomes we expect to gain from our lives.
- There are three ways of focusing that we can choose in life's variety of situations: 1. Expecting to fail; 2. Trying not to fail; and 3. Expecting success.
- The brain works teleologically: it moves towards what it is focused upon. It therefore creates the outcomes that dominate our thoughts, good, bad or indifferent.
- The brain cannot differentiate between a 'do' and a 'don't' so will gravitate towards negative results as easily as it will to successful ones.
- It is essential, therefore, that we focus on what we do want, not what we don't want.

SECTION TWO

THE IMPORTANCE OF WHAT YOU THINK ABOUT YOU

"We're all on a journey to
Finding the real inner you"
Goldfrapp, "Happiness", Seventh Tree

Having spent some time considering how we think and the variety of ways we can focus in a range of circumstances, it is time to change tack and spend some time on another topic; the importance of what you think about yourself.

As an opener, consider the following:

You have just been introduced to someone at a social function and asked to describe the kind of person you think you are. If you were to answer this inquiry with the use of the phrase "I am the sort of person who..." how would you complete your reply?

From the many thousands of people I have met over the years I have heard a wide range of responses. For example:

"I am the sort of person who...

- likes to work in sales
- likes to read Shakespeare
- enjoys the outdoor life
- loves having fun
- worries too much
- never feels in control of his life
- gets stressed and angry easily
- tries always to be the life and soul of the party"

Do you see, or hear, yourself somewhere in this list? What would you say in this situation?

You may well be asking why this matters. Why should the way we view or consider ourselves be of any importance to the life we enjoy or endure?

Let's try to answer this question by using the example of something that we have all come across: a thermostat on a central heating system. Most of us will have or have had one of these in our homes or in our workplaces, usually tucked away in a corner or in a hallway.

It is quite straightforward and not unusual to set a thermostat at 20 degrees centigrade. If the sensor in the device is activated, when the temperature falls below this mark a signal will automatically be sent to the boiler and the heating system will be turned on. When the required temperature is reached the system will turn itself off again.

It is the thermostat that does our programmed bidding, but we as human beings decide the parameters on which it will operate.

In a very similar way we decide for ourselves what we think and believe about ourselves and this creates our own self-image. This self-image in turn determines the level of self-esteem we enjoy or, perhaps, do not.

You could say, then, that your self-image is in fact your own personal thermostat.

If we think about ourselves in a particular and consistent way over time, these repeated thoughts will develop into hard and fast, concrete beliefs about ourselves.

But let's just slow down for a while and make sure that we are clear about the terms being used here as we have come quite a distance fairly quickly.

What exactly do we mean by a "belief"?

In simple terms a belief is something that you accept as either true or real.

Your self-image, which could also be termed your personal identity, is composed of many beliefs you have about yourself.

These beliefs, and the self-image that accrues from them, are what, in turn, create your own personal limitations.

So, how, in the real world, does this exhibit itself?

If, for example, you strongly believe that you are the sort of person who just can't get a job, what do you think is the probable consequence of this way of thinking? You're right: prolonged periods of unemployment.

In turn, how will you be feeling? Like a person who will only know failure.

How will you be behaving? Like a person who might as well give up as nothing can be gained from any effort.

What are the long term consequences? Poverty, unhappiness, lack of fulfillment.

On the other end of the scale, let's consider someone who strongly believes they will be fully employed and earning £500k next year.

Consider the same questions above. What different kinds of answers do you think you will find?

Let's get some perspective on this. It's not just about money and career ambition. I have met lots of people who would love to enjoy the fruits that are missing from some area of their lives, such as a long-term loving relationship, the ability to organise their lives effectively, to achieve more in the sporting arena or to be more productive and efficient in their jobs. Unfortunately they have also believed that they will not achieve them.

At this point I would ask you again to consider some of the ideas I have just mentioned and any others that may have sprung into your mind. What are the beliefs you have about yourself and your own potential and what is holding you back in certain, specific areas of your life?

It may be worthwhile to refer yourself back at this juncture to your own performance audit that you carried out earlier (see the Foundation Section) to remind yourself of some of the issues that you identified.

So where do we go from here?

Clearly it is possible for us to identify our personal delimiting beliefs and behaviour quite readily, but the question that follows is what can we do about this? How can we work on and change this belief system to bring about an adapted and evolved self-image that will bring us more attractive and enjoyable outcomes in our lives?

It's not a simple task. All of us will have had years of early life in which we will have been drip-fed regular and consistent ideas, attitudes and beliefs from a wide range of other people, including family, friends and teachers. As young and immature human beings we readily adopted and assimilated these beliefs as our own and unquestioningly accepted them as we developed into adulthood.

But this isn't necessarily the end of the story. While we can't control the influences that others exerted upon us either purposefully or unwittingly in the past, we can most definitely start to be more in control of what we are drip-feeding our minds within the present.

Let me tell you about an old lady that I knew personally.

This agreeable and uncomplaining woman had a very large family that was geographically dispersed and personally disparate. She was invited to weddings, funerals and other events that involved one or more of its members on a regular basis. Because of her relationship to these people, she felt obligated to attend even though this was very often not what she really wanted to do. She would have felt guilty not to have done so. What she was doing was fulfilling a rather empty role at the expense of her real feelings. She told me that one day she had a forceful realisation that she did not have to keep on doing this. The power actually rested with her and not the other distant members of her family. So, when she received her RSVP invitations she felt comfortable to say, "Thank you but no thank you".

This anecdote leads us into the field of language and psycholinguistics or what can be called more simply and comfortably our self-talk – the words and phrases that we use to both ourselves and others every single day.

Shad Helmstetter, an expert in this area, has come to the conclusion from his research activities that for up to 70% of our waking hours we are indulging in some kind of self-talk. This self-talk can exist on three levels: Primary Questions, Informal Self-Talk and Formal Self-Talk. Let me expand upon what these represent:

Primary Questions
In any set of circumstances we regularly ask ourselves questions and the nature of these questions plays a great part in our subsequent mental and emotional states.

For example, in considering an action or a task we might ask ourselves:

- "Why do I always mess things up?"
- "How can I have been so useless?"
- "Why do I always run out of time?"
- "Why do I get so nervous?"

However, if we recognise the steering quality of the mind, we can see how these may reinforce negative images of ourselves and, as a result, decide to rephrase and restructure them in more constructive and positive forms:

- "What can I learn from my performance today?"
- "How can I plan in advance to ensure that I use all of my time efficiently?"
- "What can I do to bring about better results in that area?"

Informal Self-Talk
Often we define ourselves to ourselves in negative ways:

- "I'm always late…"
- "I can't do…"
- "I'm just a clumsy person"
- "I'm rubbish at that"

But we could move ourselves towards more beneficial outcomes by expressing ourselves in a more positive fashion:

- "I'm getting better at this"
- "I can find a way"
- "I'm really improving at…"
- "I was great today!"

Formal Self-Talk

We can take major steps towards redefining our self-image over time by the use of affirmations or deliberately constructed sentences designed to generate a positive belief in the achievement of written goals.

As a general principle, this formal language will prove to be most effective when it is expressed in the following way:

Personal – About you – use the first person "I"
Present tense – Reality happens now
Positive – Expressed in terms of what you want not what you don't want

For example:
"I am a good salesperson who gives excellent customer service"

To put a human face on this, let me tell you a brief story about a woman I met who desperately wanted to become a partner in the accountancy firm she worked for. Unfortunately, despite this deep desire, the truth was that she could not honestly see herself in this role. She just could not conjure up the image of how she would be in this lofty position. Working with her over a period of time, creating and establishing affirmations and changing her personal "thermostat" settings, we were able to help her visualise this change in her own self-image. Within one year she had achieved her ambition and more. She had actually been head-hunted by another firm and was absolutely delighted to accept their offer.

So let's end this section with an action point.

Having thought about what you would like to improve or enhance about your current performance in whatever field or arena, put together six formally constructed self-talk affirmations using the template above.

Every morning and every evening take a few minutes to read them aloud to yourself.

YOUR SELF PSYCHOLOGY SECTION TWO KEY POINTS

- Most of us can say quite easily what we think we are good and not so good at without too much thought. This is often in the form of "I am the sort of person who…"
- These statements about ourselves need to be analysed carefully as they reveal self-limiting beliefs that we have about ourselves.
- It is quite easy to see how this kind of self talk provides a window on what we hold to be our

self-image, or personal "thermostat", which in turn dictates the levels of self-esteem we enjoy or suffer from.

- These "beliefs" about ourselves – meaning things that we hold to be true – are powerful psychological phenomena and it is immensely valuable to be able to recognise and acknowledge what these are and the effect they may be having.

- Psychologists have suggested that for about 70% of our time we involve ourselves in what is termed "self-talk" – the words and phrases we use about ourselves. There are three levels of self-talk. These are Primary Questions, Informal Self-Talk and Formal Self-Talk.

- There are many ways of taking action to change and improve our individual self-image.

- This can be done through the use of affirmations about ourselves written in a carefully constructed fashion and read aloud to ourselves every day.

SECTION THREE

TAKING PERSONAL RESPONSIBILITY

"Let X=X. You know, it could be you."

Laurie Anderson, "Let X=X", Big Science

Once again, let us make sure that we define our terms. If we are going to talk meaningfully about personal responsibility, we must first come to an agreement about what we understand by this important term.

What does it mean to be personally responsible? If someone is personally responsible, she or he is willingly and totally accountable for her or his actions and behaviour. This is not, however, a state of affairs that has to be imposed on an individual. A truly personally responsible human being is one who conducts her or himself consistently according to an internally defined set of well-considered and principled guidelines.

In this chapter we will examine how this desirable situation can be achieved. However, I would first like to point out just how easy it is to detect those who have not yet made this decisive step. You may not have realised this, but it is really quite simple to do.

When people are unwilling to take full responsibility for their actions or choices, there are several familiar, recurring phrases that they are likely to use and that you will quickly recognise, such as:

- "It's just fate—there's nothing I can do about it"
- "I'm always in debt—these credit cards make it far too easy to spend money"
- "It's your fault, you should have reminded me!"
- "I'm constantly overweight because people keep bringing cakes to work"

Thinking and speaking in this way has potentially very unhelpful and, indeed, quite damaging consequences. As we have seen in earlier chapters, the repetitive, drip-feed effect of negative thinking can lead to feelings of hopelessness and disempowerment because underlying all these utterances is the implication that somewhere there is someone or something, and it's definitely not you, who is responsible for your choices and your actions.

This is a vital lesson to learn. It is only by taking full personal responsibility for our actions that we can truly begin to grow, develop new skills, respect ourselves more, raise our confidence levels and consequently attain positive improvements in our self-image and self-esteem.

At this point it might be worthwhile to pause and check if all this is coming as a shock or challenge to you. Reading this chapter may be raising a few hackles for you as you say to yourself, "But I just don't have control over everything!"

I would agree—you don't. But what you do have for certain is more control over your life and yourself than you may have realised up to this juncture.

So let me make the point loudly and clearly once more by flipping things over and showing you why not taking responsibility for your own life and choices is ultimately so damaging for you.

If you are not happy with your life, or some important part of it, but you are unwilling to acknowledge and own the choices you have made and the actions you have taken that have had important parts to play in the way that things have turned out, then what you are doing is externalising where the force and responsibility lie. In this mindset, the power behind your life lies somewhere out there. The logical consequence of this form of thinking is to go on believing that the only thing that can make your life better is some external force. However, the truth is that if you are waiting to be rescued from your problems by luck, fate or another person, you may be waiting a very, very long time.

I would contend strongly that always being responsible for your own actions and choices is one of the highest forms of human maturity. Very successful people and consistently high performers do not tend to blame others for where they are. They know that their personal outcomes are entirely down to them.

So here are two crucial questions:

- How personally responsible are you?
- How much personal responsibility do you take for your choices and actions?

But let's be careful here. At this point, I need to add a cautionary note. There is something that you should be wary of.

Over the years I have met a lot of people who would like to *think* that they are very personally responsible and have told me so with complete conviction. Some have been right, but others have been nowhere near as close to this state of being as they would like to believe.

Some still come out with telltale phrases like:

- "I have to…"
- "I must…"
- "I have no choice."
- "It's inevitable that…"
- "I really should, but…"

Despite their protestations, this kind of language tells us all loud and clear that these people are still willing to externalise where the responsibility lies for their own actions.

So let's take yet another step.

How would you respond to these questions?

Do you have to:

- Obey the law?
- Turn up for work tomorrow, as per usual, if you have a job?
- Continue reading this book now you've started?

- Drive your children around, if you have them, week after week to school, parties, sports activities?
- Pay your next monthly mortgage or rent instalment?
- Work late next Friday evening as this would be very useful to your organisation?

I would predict with some confidence that your initial reaction to most of these would be to say "Yes".

I would suggest to you, however, that the very opposite of what you are saying is true. In reality you don't have to do any of these things. There are consequences if you do and consequences if you don't. It's all about you.

Whether you choose to do these things or not is being driven by what I would call your "choice drivers", which we all, in our own individual ways, have evolved and which consist of an amalgam of our values, beliefs, conscience and level of awareness. In turn these have created our emotional needs and desires in, and for, our lives.

You can see after all the work we have done together so far, that these choice drivers are elements of our own thinking. I would put it to you that in every action you take and every choice you make you are, in some way, seeking to satisfy your own choice drivers and, as a consequence, your own emotional needs.

It should be clear by now that there is no need or use in blaming others for our own actions, or ever moaning, whingeing or complaining about what it is we're doing or where we are.

This is not to say, though, that making choices and choosing actions in life are always pleasant and enjoyable things to do. There may well be times when we are faced by very challenging sets of circumstances and the options open to us are all difficult and, perhaps, unpleasant.

The example of an estate agent I knew in the 1980s is a useful one:

This young man had already worked hard to build up a small chain of estate agencies with a couple of business partners who were all enjoying the economic boom that surrounded them at that time. So successful were they that they were soon approached by a national company that made them a very lucrative offer for their business, one which would have secured their financial futures for life. The three discussed the matter fully and, after some deliberation, decided against the move. Within two years the property market had crashed and their company had folded. The individual in question could have spent the rest of his life ruing his actions and enduring long years of bitter regret. Fortunately he made the choice not to do this. He knew that he had made his own decision and chose to live with it. He had a great deal to reflect upon and to learn but he was not bitter.

What we can best do at times like these is to work within the testing parameters that face us and choose the action that is less nasty or injurious than the others. For example, if one day you find yourself a little shorter of money than you expected, you might need to decide between taking a holiday, buying some new clothes, having some repairs done on the house or updating the car. You may feel you need to do all of these but just decide which is the most important and the most pressing. It's not any kind of sacrifice, just a requirement to make the best rational decision you can.

Here are three recommendations to help you enhance your level of personal responsibility:

1. Work to eradicate the thinking and language of helplessness. Thinking you "have to" and blaming others will never serve you well.

2. Replace this with the thinking and language of personal responsibility and empowerment–"I am…", "I'm going to…", "It's me".

3. Take a higher quality and more personally responsible you with you wherever you go and make even more of the place that you put yourself in.

In other words just Let X=X.

YOUR SELF PSYCHOLOGY SECTION THREE
KEY POINTS

- To be successful in life, an individual needs to take full responsibility for his or her actions, behaviours and choices.
- It is easy to spot those who have not understood this in their lives by listening closely to the language that they use to express their situations. In life there are no real *have to*'s or *got to*'s, there is only our human power to choose. By taking responsibility for our choices and actions we are able to grow, develop new skills, respect ourselves more, raise our confidence levels and consequently attain positive improvements in our self-image and self-esteem.
- In short, it can be argued that accepting personal choice is one of the highest forms of human maturity.
- It is very easy to externalise the forces that shape your life and blame others or circumstances for your situation. If this were the case then the only way life could improve

would be if some outside force came along and provided a solution.

- What we decide to do is driven by our choice drivers, our psychological process of identifying and selecting options, which in turn are the products of our thinking.

- To improve we can decide to take steps to change our language and our thinking to express ourselves in positive and personally responsible ways.

Your Life
Psychology

SECTION ONE

THE IMPORTANCE OF YOUR ATTITUDE

"Let your little light shine"

Joni Mitchell, "Shine", Shine

There is an obvious problem with writing about attitude. It is a difficult word to pin down because it has such a range of meanings and cultural connotations. It is important, therefore to define from the start what this word will denote within this context.

Your attitude is an established, perhaps even engrained, way of thinking and/or behaving. It is a consolidated expression of your particular view of your place in the world around you.

So why does it matter so much? Sir Winston Churchill was of the opinion that "Attitude is a little thing that makes a big difference". Let's use the great man's wise words to examine how this state of mind may have an influence on your performance health.

Let me start by asking you a question. Do you ever have moments when you take part in what could be called "I'll be happy when..." type thinking. And perhaps also:

- "I'll be relieved when..."
- "I'll be able to relax when..."
- "I'll start to enjoy myself when...."

If you do, do you think that this is the best way of creating a sense of happiness or contentment for yourself?

If you take only a brief moment to consider what is happening here, you will soon see that you are relying heavily upon what is just a hoped-for future set of conditions or state of being. All that you are doing is tossing a ball hopefully into the playing field of the future and banking on the chance that it will land in a favourable spot.

"What's so wrong with that?" you might ask. "Isn't a good idea for us all to be hoping optimistically for a better future?"

On one very limited level, of course I would agree. I would certainly advocate looking forward to particular things in life. There is absolutely nothing wrong with that at all. But there is a very big difference between simply looking forward to something and intentionally putting your entire emotional state on hold until some future, unspecified moment.

I have already highlighted the indisputable fact that most people want and would like to strive towards some degree of happiness, fulfillment or satisfaction in their lives. However, if your psychological approach to this is to put things off until some fictional future moment when everything falls into place, the planets align or your boat finally decides to come in, you are very unlikely to experience emotionally what it is you are looking for.

So, if hoping against hope that happiness will come knocking at our door at some future date is not the answer, then what can or should you be doing?

I can assure you that there are other far more effective, psychologically-based ways of moving yourself towards a happier and more fulfilling state, but let me make a couple of important distinctions within this, between the longer term and the here and now.

The first thing I would ask is that you spend some considerable time thinking about what you really want from and in your life. When you believe that you have clearly identified your true ambitions, the next step is to set clear and achievable goals for yourself. We will be looking at how to do this in greater detail in the second section of "Your Life Psychology". When you achieve these goals, I recommend that you experience maximum pleasure from accomplishing what you set out to do.

This really is the icing that is available to put on top of this particular cake; a notion of genuine happiness which is quite different from those faulty examples we mentioned earlier. Happiness is a choice. It's something that we should, and can, work to create not just in the future but in the background of our lives every day.

For happiness is not a place, it is a way of being. It is not a destination but a decision about the way we want to be. In the view of 17th century moralist Roger L'Estrange, "It is not the place, nor the condition, but the mind alone that can make anyone happy or miserable."

Abraham Lincoln, himself quite an extraordinary human being, once said, "People are about as happy as they make up their minds to be," and I believe that we should learn from his simple but insightful words.

To test these ideas out let's just take a short trip back to Chapter One, Section One, where we paid attention to what people often call "That Monday morning feeling". For some this sinking feeling lasts for just half an hour; for others it may persist for the whole day or even well beyond. In extreme cases it may nag away at them until Friday evening finally arrives.

If we refresh the points from this earlier chapter, we will remember that it is the repetitious, drip-feeding effect of the conscious mind that infiltrates and occupies the subconscious and hence our emotional state. It becomes, in other words, our attitude.

Now, let me ask you a serious question. Is this really how you want to spend your life? Is this, truly, how you want to feel? I think I already know the answer to both of these questions: no, of course not.

Let's explore this a little further.

There are 1,440 minutes in a day—the most valuable resource you will ever be blessed with.

Sadly, most people take them completely for granted.

If you were to be given something that you were really striving for – let's say a luxury home or a brand new Ferrari – but tragically your daily 1,440 minutes were taken away, would these material things be of any real use to you?

Clearly they wouldn't. A huge bank account, a wardrobe of expensive designer clothes or any kind of material possessions are meaningless paraphernalia without time and life itself to enjoy them.

By the same token, if we really worked hard at our attitude, if we adjusted the way we think about time itself, we wouldn't waste our mental, emotional and physical energies creating this doom-laden and life-denying Monday morning phenomenon.

If you really do hate your job so much that this is what your life has become, then you have two choices open to you. Either change the job you have or change your attitude to it. It really is as simple as that. As Denis Waitley, author of *The Psychology of Winning*, says, "There are two primary choices in life: to accept conditions as they exist, or accept the responsibility for changing them."

If you do want to enhance the attitude you have to your life, one powerful thing I would recommend that you do is create a Gratitude Journal.

Appreciation and gratitude are two of the highest forms of emotional experience. When you are appreciating something you create the sort of emotional experience that most people strive for. Sometimes people refer to this emotional experience as genuine happiness.

Step back and take a look across the full spectrum of your life and compare those areas of your life that you would dearly like to improve upon and those parts which are truly brilliant. You will see that the positive aspects of your life that you should be truly grateful for far outweigh the more negative aspects that you can become distressed about. Yet which do you spend most of your waking hours preoccupied by?

To repeat, if there are unachieved ambitions in your life, then set out your goals and work hard towards attaining them. Whilst you are doing this, remember that there are many things to be genuinely thankful for. If you don't, as yet, believe this, take part in the following activity:

Take a blank piece of paper, sit down, relax and consciously identify those things, large or small, that you know that you can feel grateful for. As they come to you, write them down. They can be about anything you like—healthy children, a roof over your head, paid work, good friends...

Do this regularly as a written exercise and keep the results of your honest introspection for future reference.

A Gratitude Journal really is a very helpful tool. Purposefully taking time on a regular basis to be grateful for and appreciate what is valuable in your life is a special habit to develop and will bring you more positive focus. It will also often bring a smile to your face.

YOUR LIFE PSYCHOLOGY SECTION ONE KEY POINTS

- Your attitude is an established, perhaps even engrained, way of thinking and/or behaving. It is a consolidated expression of your particular view of your place in the world around you.
- It is common to find many individuals who habitually base their happiness on some future set of conditions or state.
- Happiness is really a choice that we make. It's something that we should, and can, work to create not just in the future but in the background of our lives every day.
- Time, the 1,440 minutes we have every day, is the most valuable resource that we will ever have. Respect it and spend it in worthwhile ways for you.

- Some people are given to complaining about their lives, but it is up to each one of us to make the choices that are available to us. There are two primary choices in life: to accept conditions as they exist, or accept the responsibility for changing them
- Instead of spending long hours focusing upon those parts of our lives that are not working well, it would be better to concentrate attention upon those areas that are good or working well and that we should feel appreciation and gratitude for.
- Writing a Gratitude Journal is a great way to make this happen on a regular basis.
- For those areas of life that are not working so well, spend some time thinking about what you really want, set goals and take action.

SECTION TWO

HOLISTIC GOAL SETTING

*"Are you hungry for a little more
than what you've had before?
Are you hungry for a taste of life
to whet your appetite?"*

Kosheen, "Hungry", Resist

Here's a very interesting statistic for you. In the UK, apparently, only 3% of adults regularly set formal goals for their lives outside the workplace.

How crazy is this? I know of very few people who cannot supply you with an answer if you ask them if there are things they would like to do or achieve in their lives ahead. Many will give you a list of dreams and ambitions.

So why is it, then, if our lives and drives are so obviously important to us, that we pay so little attention, and give so little energy, to what we really want to create, achieve and enjoy?

I believe that the answer to this conundrum can be gleaned from an examination of the kind of excuses we have all come across at various times:

- *"I've got enough to do in my life without having to think about all that."*
- *"If you don't set goals for yourself, then you don't have to worry about the chance of failing."*
- *"I'm just too busy at the moment."*
- *"How can I control my life when I spend all my time looking after everyone else?"*
- *"I don't even know what's happening tomorrow, let alone for the next year or two!"*

By now, you may well be able to spot the underlying nature of these comments and the responses they evoke in anyone who has taken the time to seriously consider how they are really conducting their lives. Do we honestly want to look back over the years and be filled with regret for what we might have done, what we should have done or what, in our heart of hearts, we know we could have done?

In this chapter, then, we will address a simple but hugely important matter that takes us further along the road to creating and enjoying the lives that we really want for ourselves.

Whether we are 20 or 70 there are still things that all of us would like to create or achieve. The choice remains as to whether we sit back, cross our fingers and wait for these things to mysteriously drop into our laps or whether we take control and galvanise the amazing piece of kit that we call our brain to create, in a conscious and positive fashion, the future we hunger to experience.

I believe that setting personal goals is a vital and major step towards achieving this ambition.

*

Before we move on to the way we can successfully achieve this, let's examine the how too many people approach their life and self-improvement.

A good example is what happens every year in the first couple of weeks of January. Many people set themselves New Year's resolutions, often with a half-hearted, "Well, I suppose I'd better..." attitude, and these vague pieces of wishful thinking generally result in little action and less achievement.

What, precisely, is it that makes these utterances feel so very anaemic? The answer is that there is an absence of two fundamental ingredients: Positive Belief and Strong Desire.

Having worked closely with many thousands of individuals over recent years, I know that the majority of high performing, very successful and most personally fulfilled people regularly set themselves goals for their lives. There is such a common and pronounced link between the two that the message is clear: if you truly want to join the ranks of these people, set yourself goals and do so in a robust and methodical fashion.

*

If you need any more convincing, take a look at some examples from history and the present day of people who have achieved hugely in their lives. Do you really think that the Wright brothers, Roger Bannister, Richard Branson or Bill Gates would have got where they did without having clear and precise goals?

Take yourself back to Your Self Psychology, Section One and remind yourself of what was said about the teleological nature of the brain. Remember that it is a natural function and it is no coincidence or accident that the mind gravitates inexorably towards the goals that it has set for itself. Remember, too, Steven Covey's famous recommendation to "always start with the end in mind" and consider carefully the full implications of these words.

Before we even attempt the beneficial task of setting ourselves goals, I want you to take some time to create a clarity within which you can carefully consider the current situation of your life. It is important to break down this picture into manageable chunks and identify exactly what is going on.

A useful tool to help you complete this task is what I call a Life Audit, which you will find below and which you can conduct for yourself three or four times a year. Ask yourself whether the identified areas of your life have high, medium or low importance to you and then give each a score out of ten in order to clarify just how satisfied you are with this element of your life at this time.

MindSpan Life Audit

Area of life	Tick if important to you	Satisfaction Score out of 10
Career	☐	☐
Work	☐	☐
Finance	☐	☐
Family	☐	☐
Health	☐	☐
Fitness	☐	☐
Travel	☐	☐
Home	☐	☐
Domestic Relationships	☐	☐
Social Relationships	☐	☐
Work Relationships	☐	☐
Hobbies and Leisure	☐	☐
Personal Challenge	☐	☐
Education/Learning	☐	☐
Community	☐	☐
Material	☐	☐

One of the obvious and immediate benefits of conducting this exercise is the ready insight that it gives you into what is working well in your life and what requires new focus and improvement. You might call this Stage 1, or how things are at the moment.

Stage 2, as you start to consider and decide where you would like all these elements of your life to be, should begin by focusing on the areas where you scored low satisfaction. For each of these, I would like you to paint a mental picture of what each of those parts of your life would look like if you were to give it a maximum score of 10.

From this, write a "word picture" of each of these areas. This word picture needs to include images that portray clearly what you would be doing, how you would be feeling and where you would be, with whom, doing what, etc. This may take a little time to complete as this personal visualisation must be very clear; the quality of the content that you construct here will inform the direction and purpose behind the well-constructed goals that you go on to create.

Once you have clearly defined your mental destinations, you can go on to formulate the goals that you wish to set for yourself. Once again, much thought is needed to do this in the most effective manner. Based on many years of research and practice, I have found that the following goal-setting method is the most powerful you can adopt to maximise your outcomes.

I call this The 4x4 Method and it requires you to produce written goals.

Your written goals should be:

1. Expressed personally using the personal pronouns "I" or "We"
2. Written in the present tense as if the goal has just been or already achieved
3. With the outcome desired clearly defined
4. With the precise date by which your goal is to be achieved included

These four elements are supported by you, in daily practice, by:

1. Your positive belief
2. Your strong desire
3. Your positive self-talk
4. Your positive visualisation

In my experience, when individuals really buy into this systematic approach their rates of achievement really do improve quite markedly.

So let me explain why I believe this methodology to be so important and effective.

Writing personally and using the first person pronoun creates a psychological and emotional connection that reinforces your responsibility for the achievement of the goal.

The key importance of *writing goals in the present tense* allows the writer to really see him or herself right there amidst the outcome that is desired. There is a strong psychological link created between the idea and the visualisation of its achievement using this approach.

Clearly defining the outcomes responds to the human brain's inability to respond well to vagueness of thought and expression. On the contrary, clarity and precision excite and satisfy the mind. So there is a great deal of difference in the impact made by *hoping* to "travel" one day and *planning* to "go to India with my family in December of next year".

Specifying the date of achievement is of central importance because the vague and wishful notion that you will do what you want to do "one day" is so nebulous that, as we are all aware, it will rarely ever happen. Having a deadline works to galvanise you to take action and turn mere dreams into solid and achievable realities.

In support of these, it is equally important to foreground the four driving forces that will energise the task of fulfilling these well-made goals.

Earlier, we defined a *belief* as something that you hold to be true or real. Many people have told me that goals need to be what they term "realistic" and, while I would not disagree with them I would also ask, exactly what is "realistic"? What to one person is obviously possible can to another seem incredibly unattainable. What appears realistic is only that which exists as believable already in our heads and that many human beings have achieved great things in the face of others warning them repeatedly that they could not be done. Very often it is a powerful act to challenge positively the limits that we imagine and create for ourselves.

Desire is a trait that is weak or missing in many people. Often we say we want things but don't really feel like making the effort needed to bring these to fruition. It is equally obvious that we could set our sights much higher than we often choose to. There is nothing inherently wrong with leading an average life but, this may not be what we really want. Successful people are often those who display the most evident levels of personal desire and the stronger our desire, the more we will take action to overcome obstacles and fulfill our personal ambitions.

Earlier in this book, we discussed and emphasised the primary importance of positive *self-talk*. I do want to re-emphasise that it is essential that you consistently talk to yourself and others in terms which confirm and reinforce your ability to achieve your goals.

The use of *positive visualisation* is well known to be a powerful performance tool. Watching a top-class high jumper preparing to run up and leap is a very good example of this. Recent discoveries about how the brain works have given us greater understanding of just how powerful the impact of this technique can be. Whenever we imagine and visualise ourselves in a certain place, at a certain time, having a certain experience we now know that our subconscious mind and our central nervous system respond as if we were in fact really there. What this means is that at a subconscious level we cannot distinguish between a real and a clearly imagined experience and the simple logic of this is that the more we imagine ourselves achieving our goals at high levels, the more we programme our subconscious to create these events in reality.

Moreover regular visualisation can actually strengthen this supportive circle by confirming our *belief* that things are indeed possible and by deepening our *desire* to achieve them.

Having identified and explored the robust nature of The 4X4 Method, let us use this knowledge to produce some well-constructed goals. Here are some good examples:

"It is the 12th of December (year) and I am with my family in Machu Pichu. The scenery and surroundings are astonishing and it feels wonderful to be sharing this with the people I love most."

"It is August 22nd (year) and I have just received the letter containing my A Level results that mean I am on my way to Oxford for the next three years of my student life."

"It is the end of March (year) and I have exceeded my sales targets by 30%. I have been more focused this year and have a large bonus of £???? to invest for my family."

Can you think of and produce goals in a similar fashion for yourself?

When you have completed this, write them down on cards, in a journal or notebook. As a basic minimum, you should say these aloud to yourself for two or three minutes first thing in the morning and again just before you retire for the night. In terms of the time you have available to you in your everyday life this is a very small investment.

However the effect of the consistent and repetitive nature of these personal efforts is immensely important. By acting in this way your goals will be drilled down into your subconscious, strengthening your focus upon them and igniting your teleological brain in ways that are likely to maximise your chances of achievement and personal fulfillment. You can enhance this daily routine even further by engaging in the visualisation of your goals at the point of achievement. This is a heady combination of concurrent and mutually sustaining activities.

*

Our lives are always the consequence of our accumulated thinking, behaviours and associated habits. These can be difficult to change if they are not properly addressed.

A friend of mine found himself in a difficult situation when his career and colleagues led him to become driven in a way that began to present a real danger to himself and his family. He was spending a great deal of time away from home in London hotels and neglecting those close to him as a result. Despite what might outwardly seem to be his professional success he had, he realised, come to a point where he lacked clarity about his life and what he wanted from it. After conducting his own Life Audit he made a change and bought a small property in London. This not only made him feel better personally, but also allowed him to bring his family with him at times to share the big city experience and thus preserve their regular contact. For him, making this small decision to audit his life preserved his marriage and led to improved lifestyles for both him and all the others around him that he treasured.

At the end of this chapter on setting personal goals, I invite you to take stock and consider carefully the combined effect of The 4x4 Method of setting goals, and the immense potential these goals have to motivate and bring about the desired outcomes. Make this an integral part of your life and a habit as regular as cleaning your teeth. You will reap the huge benefits that are waiting to be enjoyed.

YOUR LIFE PSYCHOLOGY SECTION TWO KEY POINTS

- Only around 3% of us set ourselves formal goals in our personal lives—an incredibly low figure when we consider that virtually all of us have strong ambitions about what we want to have or achieve.

- If we want to achieve these things, it is advisable for us to construct formally recorded goals written in a very specific fashion.

- Before attempting this it is beneficial to complete a Life Audit so as to gain total clarity and a better understanding of where we feel we are at this time.

- Once this is done it is valuable to begin the process of visualising the improvements in our lives that we want to see.

- To construct goals that will drive us forward to their realisation, use the 4x4 method of goal setting.

- Once you have constructed these goals, commit to writing them down on cards, keep them visible and read them aloud at appropriate moments each day.

- This process, when adopted as a normal daily practice, is hugely beneficial as it starts to programme the sub-conscious for our personal success.

Your World
Psychology

SECTION ONE

EMOTIONAL SELF-MANAGEMENT (OR ARE YOU FEELING AS GOOD AS YOU COULD?)

*"Life is bigger
It's bigger than you...*

*

Consider this, consider this..."

R.E.M., "Losing My Religion", *Out Of Time*

If you ever take the time to ask people what they want from their lives, their responses are interesting and very informative.

There are as many answers as there are individuals who offer them, but more often than not they include jobs, houses, cars, children, good causes and other worthy areas of human endeavour and desire.

What they all have in common is that people want these things because of the way they believe that they will make them feel. Generally, we want to feel good and often we want to feel much better than we actually do.

In fact everything we do is in some way designed to meet our emotional needs—to make us feel better, to move away from pain in its various forms or towards pleasure in a range of guises—we want to feel good!

If this is the case, why are there so many people who are so stressed, angry and frustrated in their daily lives? What is it that's happening to them to bring about this state of affairs? Where on earth is all this stress coming from?

Let's step back and take some time to consider these questions for ourselves.

First of all I want to tell you about a police officer I met some time ago at a course I was delivering. He was feeling the pressure of his job very badly at the time, working long hours and returning home in a distressed and agitated frame of mind. Waiting for him there was a wife and two young children and, invariably, a messy house with toys, clothes and other sundries scattered around. This was too much for him to bear and he frequently found himself losing his temper and channelling his anger at his wife and family whose "fault" it was for making him feel this way. After one day of working with him on his emotional self-management, he was able to make a remarkable change.

On his return home the next day, he found that there was the usual disorder and, in addition, no dinner to be had. Instead of blowing his top as he might have done before, the policeman took a very different path. Speaking calmly to his wife he told her there was absolutely no problem and instead he wanted to thank her for all the work that she had put in that day, and every day, for the children and their family as a whole. Thankfully he had managed to recognise the nature and extent of his own stressed mind and taken positive steps to reframe his view and understanding of the world around him.

So, to expand this inquiry further, here's a simple question: what are some of the things that you get stressed about? Find a pen and write down briefly what makes you angry, frustrated or distressed.

Have a look at the list below:-

- Bad drivers
- Rudeness
- Politicians
- Disobedient children
- Broken promises
- Untidiness
- The weather

Have you included any of these?

Here's what I would suggest you to do. Press the stop button on all of this now! There is an awakening that I strongly encourage you to make for yourself.

Consider this...

Realise that from this point on in your life, you will always have options in terms of the way you decide to respond to the items that you have put on the list you have just made. Your options are as follows:

1. You can make no change – just go on reacting and responding in exactly the same way you always have done and as a consequence continue to be as angry and frustrated as you usually are.

2. Challenge yourself to get out of your usual comfort zone and take action to eradicate, alleviate or eliminate the things on your list. As a consequence, although it's not always going to be easy, you will begin to feel more empowered and many of these situations will begin to improve or disappear.

This needs some further thought and exploration and we can do this by examining a possible scenario.

Let's suggest, for example, an instance of someone letting you down.

If this happens, what can you do? What are the choices open to you?
Some options are:

A. Raise it with them—and let them know how you let down you feel.
B. Ask them about it and request that it doesn't happen again.
C. Let them know how important this has been as an issue for you.
D. Decide not to rely on that person as much as you did.
E. Decide not to have anything to do with them again.

These and other options, too, are all available to you if you feel strongly enough about what has happened to take action in an empowering way. Of course, there is, as always, no absolute guarantee that any of these will work to improve things but, regardless of the potential outcome, what will be happening is that you will be taking action and behaving in a more proactive fashion. As a result you will be making, potentially, a positive impact upon the situation at hand.

3. You can consciously decide to change the way you think about the person or the situation and adopt a very different perceptual position. We call this "reframing"

Again this option requires some careful thinking through. If, for instance you get stressed about the way that another person drives then stop and consider how it could be possible to "reframe" these thoughts and feelings.

To start with it's obvious to most of us that other drivers are very unlikely to have woken up and consciously made the decision to abandon all attempts at using their indicators today just to wind us and other road-users up. If they have failed to do something that you expected from them, the likelihood is that they have just made a mistake and that is all it has been about. So why take it so personally? After all, they are most unlikely to be aiming their actions at you specifically.

So stop and challenge yourself – how important do you make other people's behaviours? Most people aren't being untidy, failing to deliver a promise or being late just to annoy you. This is not to make excuse for other people's errors or carelessness, but the crucial issue here is how personally you want to take all this because the more you do, the more you will wind yourself up.

In our heads we all carry round what we could call "the world-according-to-me". It's what we think is right and wrong, good and bad, acceptable and unacceptable about people and the world they inhabit. In short this is our "mental map" and we all measure others by our own expectations, employing a wide spectrum of views and opinions ranging from very strong to very soft.

You and I, all of us, pay a high price for many of our strong views and opinions of others and the world around us. When the world and other mortals don't measure up to these, the toll on us is to create and feel reactions of stress, anger and frustration.

Let me share with you a very personal story to illustrate just how real and important these kinds of events can be in our lives.

My father, late in his life and without knowing consciously what he was doing, developed increasingly strong views and opinions about the world around him. As a consequence of this he became, at times, a very stressed and angry man and, needless to say, this state of affairs did not make for happy family gatherings. Sadly, in the early part of 2004, at the age of 65, he was diagnosed with a terminal illness, motor-neurone disease.

This was, of course, devastating news for him and us as a family but it brought about a quite remarkable change in him. Within a matter of days he had "reframed" many of his opinions because, quite obviously I believe, he had suddenly made a decision about what was and was not important in his life.

As a result, in his last few months, even with a terminal illness, he actually became a much calmer person. Don't believe for a second that he didn't still get stressed and angry at times about his condition, but the difference now was that he only displayed these emotions about things that he consciously decided were worth getting upset about. Other things he was able to deal with by reframing them into "softer", less strong views and expectations.

This is a key learning point for all of us. Sometimes it is really worth getting angry about events, but if we do we need to be sure that it really is worth our while to do so. Getting upset about a toilet seat being left up or clothes not being put in the laundry basket may, and perhaps should, seem insignificant compared to our feelings about poverty, child-abuse or racist bigotry, for example.

I will be eternally grateful that my father was able to adopt a mental map that enabled him to make the most of his last few months of life, but I remain slightly sad that it took the diagnosis of a terminal illness to provide the catalyst for him to be able to do this. I always loved my father and remember him being an incredibly proud man with what he considered to be very high personal standards. It was, ironically, what he called his high principles that caused him to experience so much stress and lack of tolerance in others for much of his later life.

At the end of this chapter, I would encourage you to take some time to stop and reflect. Please don't leave it to something like the onset of a terminal illness to bring you to a point of realisation where you can take a healthy perspective on life. Give it conscious thought from today and make this a decision by and for yourself.

I hope that by now you can see where the power really lies...with you. We create for ourselves our own stress and frustrations because these are all emotions produced by our own thinking. No person, thing, or situation actually makes you stressed; you do this yourself!

Challenge yourself to take action on more of the things that you really don't like or agree with—but don't necessarily become a vigilante!

In troubling situations think about your own thinking and decide for yourself how you want to think; how important you want to make what it is in front of you and how personally you want to take it. Respond consciously—whatever you do, don't fall into your old ways of habitual reaction; start to create new, more helpful habits of response.

Remember, life is bigger, so consider this…

YOUR WORLD PSYCHOLOGY SECTION ONE KEY POINTS

- Most of us want to feel good about ourselves and our lives.
- Even so, there are many people who seem to be unhelpfully stressed, angry and frustrated in what they are doing.

- If we feel this way in particular situations we have three choices available to us: 1. To go on as we are and make no change; 2. To take action to change things; 3. To change the way we think.
- This process of reconsidering and re-prioritising our thoughts about events and situations is called "re-framing".
- In all situations it is possible to decide how important we really want to make the things and events we observe around us and to respond accordingly.
- In this way we can move away from mere habitual reaction towards a more conscious, healthy response to the world around us.

SECTION TWO

RAISING THE QUALITY OF
YOUR RELATIONSHIPS

"I'm in the middle of a chain reaction"

Diana Ross, "Chain Reaction", Eaten Alive

Let me to take you back to a key message on the subject of choice earlier in this book: we human beings, in any actions that we undertake, are always attempting to satisfy ourselves emotionally in some shape or form. So, given that self-interest underpins all we do, what does this mean in the context of the relationships we create and participate in.

I'd like to take you one step further and ask some questions that form an essential starting point to this section.

- Who do you always take with you, everywhere you go?
- Who is the only person you always listen to?
- Whose life experiences are you engaged in all day, every day?

The single answer—you—to all of these is obvious, but the importance of this realisation is central to the purposes of this chapter. It is vital both to learn and recognise that each and every human being exists in his or her own peculiar bubble or personal universe and, driven by relentless self-interest, we all enact a deep and compelling need to satisfy our own internal emotional needs.

These needs or desires can express or manifest themselves in many different ways including:

- giving help to others in acts of kindness and generosity

- accumulating or collecting material artefacts
- pursuing personal or career advancement
- indulging in specific areas of experience

Uncovering the self-centred origins of all these may come as something of a shock to you, but I would ask you to take this understanding on board and let it ride gently with you. It will help you to accept that this, indeed, is the way of the human species. More importantly, I would ask you to take the time to consider the implications of this in real life when you meet others and begin to develop relationships with them.

In short, what this means is that we must be aware and act accordingly when we start making relationships that we want to function at a high level. We must step graciously and genuinely into the worlds of others; unless we try to recognise their needs and acknowledge other people's contexts, we will not be able to establish the rapport from which productive relationships take root and thrive.

It is also important to remind ourselves that we humans are predominantly social animals and need to associate with people around us. Each one of us, at some point, will need help from a variety of others on our personal journey.

The quality of our relationships plays a vital part in our smooth and effective engagement with life and our enjoyment of it.

If you look back at your life and remember a phase when things were going well, you will probably also recall that your relationships at that time were functioning well too. Conversely, the memories you have of challenging times are more than likely to contain images of dysfunctional relationships.

So if there is a direct link between the quality of our lives and the quality of our relationships then there are some questions that we should address. Firstly, how can we learn to make the new relationships we build more effective; and secondly, how can we improve the quality of our existing ones?

We need to return to the concept of our mental maps. This "world-according-to-me" viewpoint holds our beliefs, values and what we as individuals hold to be acceptable and not acceptable.

We have already explored the effects that this mental map can have upon our emotions and day-to-day existence. However, I encourage you to be willing to acknowledge fully that we are not alone in the world and that every person we meet will be carrying around with them their own individual mental map. From early on in our lives we have the chance to observe and recognise that we all carry around a different version of this map.

So who does have the correct mental map in their head? The answer, of course, is that we all believe that our version is the right one. We are comfortable in our own minds with what we think because these thoughts are right to us and accord with the life experiences that we have encountered.

When people who are acquainted have very different mental maps, or at least differ in parts of their mental maps, and there is no willingness to appreciate or understand the other person's situation, then the quality and effectiveness of their relationship will inevitably suffer.

Judge this for yourselves. When another person is genuinely interested in you and your world, how do you feel? For the most part, you probably feel good, worthy, and valued. Of course, there are sometimes those who know this and, for their own purposes, attempt to present a false front, but most of us can recognise this. Taking a genuine interest in others and trying to assist them in their lives satisfies us, but also helps them to feel better about themselves and the world around them.

At this point I would like to take you back a step or two and ask you to consider the central question at the heart of this chapter: what are relationships for?

If this seems to be an odd question, then I suggest you take note and reflect on this. All of us take part in a variety of relationships every day of our lives. It could be argued that it is our relationships that define us as human beings, as a meaningful life would be unthinkable without them. Unfortunately, we in the western world are often very restricted in our approach to others, sticking closely to what we know or entering on only a very superficial, or often false, level into the lives of others. Even the members of our own family can seem strangers to us.

Here are two good examples of what I mean.

Many years ago, a couple I knew very well were the first among my circle of friends to buy a dishwasher. He spent a lot of time studying the manual and was convinced that he should follow the advice given to place the cutlery on the specified rack with the blades facing upwards. She, aware of the dangers that this posed for their children, was adamant that they should be put into the machine blade down. His mental map said that his way was effective and hers shouted out to her that this was dangerous. This dispute raged on between them for more than a year and I can remember whole dinner parties and social evenings being ruined by the arguments that arose from these incompatible positions.

My daughter, Emily, when young had a bedroom of her own that to my wife and me appeared to be a total and utter mess. We were constantly telling her how "untidy" it was and we would make ourselves angry in our attempts to get her to tidy it up. She did do so, but within a few days the room would return to what seemed to us its old disheveled self. It was some time before a true understanding of what was happening came to me. To us, as parents, our view of a bedroom was a place of calm and organised living which therefore needed to be tidy. According to the young Emily's mental map, her room was a place of play, discovery, excitement and learning. Both of these examples demonstrate how, as human beings, we often think quite differently about the same things. By implication, when we strongly force our view (our mental map) on others as the correct one and their view (mental map) is different, then to us it appears that theirs is the incorrect one. How do you think this makes them feel?

In summary, I believe that there can be only one answer to the question that I posed earlier. Healthy, respectful and progressive relationships exist to consolidate and enhance our lives. By making a positive impact upon the self-image and self-esteem of others, we show our incredible power to enhance their and our own well-being.

*

I strongly encourage you to become more genuinely interested in other people in general. We will focus more precisely on the kinds of behaviours and approaches that we can adopt to take the first steps in making constructive relationships with others. These can include:

- remembering their names and things of importance and interest to them
- asking them genuine questions about themselves
- concentrating and listening closely and asking further genuine questions or making appropriate comments

I once heard a footballer speaking on the radio about his memories of Sir Matt Busby, the Manager of Manchester United Football Club many years ago. He met the great man on only two occasions and there were several years between these encounters. Despite this, at their second meeting, Sir Matt walked straight up to him and asked him, by name, about the health of his daughter who had been ill when last they spoke. The footballer could only speculate as to just how many people Sir Matt must have met in the intervening years and was, as a result of this realisation, completely flabbergasted that not only had he remembered him but that he could recall their conversation in such intimate detail. Needless to say this memory of incredible human interest had a huge impact upon the player and remained a vivid memory of just how wonderful human conduct can be.

It is a truism that people like to be understood, but how can we possibly create these meaningful connections unless we enter into other people's worlds? Of course there are those who deny the need for this; "I'll start making the effort when everyone else does," is a typical response to such an idea. My response is to ask why they see such acts as an "effort". Surely this should be simply an enjoyable way of doing things. Furthermore, I would challenge this short-sighted approach with one of Steven Covey's best known quotations, "Seek first to understand before asking to be understood."

This isn't dreamy rambling or fluffy, unworldly optimism. It is just stating what is quite obvious, that these understandings are freely available to anyone sincerely interested in flourishing human relationships.

*

There is another very important understanding that we need to recognise and deal with at this point.. Lurking in the wings is a real challenge, perhaps even a threat, to the achievement of these worthy ambitions.

In our dealings with others we are seldom really objective; indeed we frequently suffer from a deep need to be right and, what's more, to be seen to be so. It would appear that there is a tendency for the human brain to search out and find solid evidence to support that which it already holds to be true. This is why all of us gravitate towards people who are like ourselves. We intuitively seek out the reassurance of similarity.

There is nothing intrinsically wrong with this inclination and behaviour. Finding others who share our views, attitudes and interests can be richly rewarding and satisfying.

In my experience when our mental map is reinforced or endorsed by others we feel:

- safe
- secure
- comfortable
- confident
- reassured
- validated

which are all connected to emotions that we desire as happy and contented human beings.

This state of affairs becomes problematic when the pursuit of the comfort of similarity is conducted at the exclusion of all other possibilities and, most importantly, the rejection of difference.

Let me explain further. Encountering difference in the people we come across can be an uncomfortable and sometimes unpleasant experience. Obviously, if we come across offensive, prejudiced and discriminatory ideas then we have the choice to walk away from what we find. However, if what we enter into is a reasonable and rational challenge to our personally held versions of what is right, then this is a different story. We can all see where these differences of world views and their attendant opinions can occur: in politics, fashion, morality, taste and so on.

Be honest here and ask yourself if you have ever found yourself uttering something like one of the following: " I wouldn't be seen dead in that…"
"That's such a train spotter thing to do…"
"The man's an idiot…"
"She's got absolutely no taste in music…"

Can you hear what is happening here? Very often when we come across difference we view it not as an alternative approach or opinion, but as a direct threat to ourselves and the mental map we not only possess but secretly cherish. Let's be clear: we don't have to agree with everyone regardless of what they say or believe; we may even want to display opposition to what these things represent. What we do need to ensure, though, is that we respect other people's right to their own mental map and the attitudes and opinions that arise from them.

If you are still not convinced, let me prove the point by painting a mental picture for you. Have you ever spent a lot of time in the presence of someone who shows a burning need to be right all the time? You can probably think of someone immediately. To them there is only one voice and only one way—theirs.

Think about it. How positively engaged do you feel in their company? This thought may bring a wry smile to your face. Fortunately, individuals who behave in this way habitually and relentlessly are few and far between, but ask yourself another question and answer honestly. Have you ever found yourself morphing into this kind of person at some time in your life? Yes? Indeed. Regrettably, perhaps, we all have.

However, while being right may be personally gratifying temporarily, it does not guarantee that we will be able to build higher quality, better functioning relationships.

Faced with this dilemma, caught between a desire to be happy in ourselves and a need to be in tune with others, how can we proceed?

Here are some ideas…

1. Be confident in your own views while not needing others to agree with you. While there is nothing wrong with wanting to be strong and safe within yourself, this does not have to depend upon your being right all the time
2. Stop needing or forcing others to see things your way and agree with the way you think. Start working at your own self-image and self-

esteem and you will have less need to have the rest of the world agree with you.

3. There doesn't have to be, and often may not be, a single way to look at any situation.

4. Take the time and make the effort to really understand the mental maps of others, particularly those close to you

5. Be self-critical. Ask questions of yourself. Why might another person be thinking that way? What can I learn about their mental map?

6. You don't have to like or agree with another person's mental map, but you do need to acknowledge their right to possess one if you want healthy relationships.

7. If you demonstrate to others an interest and understanding of their world-view it is very likely that they will more willing to do the same for you.

I would like to challenge you to raise the quality of what you control in your relationships. Think how you can show:

- understanding
- tolerance
- patience
- genuine interest
- curiosity about other people's lives
- respect

The more in control of these behaviours you are the more positive energy feeds into your relationships and the more good can be generated. I'm sure that you will have come across the expression "behaviour breeds behaviour".

You may say that all this sounds like a great deal of work and must take up a great deal of anybody's time. But let's be clear. If you want to enjoy high quality relationships there are some things that you need to bear in mind.

It is important to demonstrate mental and emotional maturity. Others will join you in this when they are ready to do so. High quality relationships are at the very heart of a happy life. Work at them and you will get out what you put in.

I encourage you to work at being more open and to embrace difference. Make a conscious effort to be genuinely and authentically interested in the world of others and be willing to be amazed by what you might learn. There is an obvious logic here: you have much more to learn from those who are different from you than those who are largely the same. Similarity is reassuring but it isn't a landscape in which to grow. Learning can only accrue from challenge, reflection and review.

My point behind all that has been said is that the deep human need to be right is the biggest obstacle to the creation and nurturing of rewarding personal relationships.

Look at anywhere in your life or in the wider world where there has been, and still is, dangerous and damaging conflict. Whether it is living with your partner, working with your colleagues, getting on with your neighbours, the situation in Northern Ireland, the Middle East—the list could go on—conflict arises and flourishes anywhere there are human beings who need to be right at the expense of someone else's deeply held need to be right too.

Ask yourself, how many of your own current relationships are consistently operating at a highly fulfilling and rewarding level.

You can only answer this for yourself, however I would very much like to reinforce the simple but extremely powerful ideas we have just examined.

Relationships hold an amazing and wonderfully beneficial potential for us all which can only be realised through our correctly considered and carefully implemented approach and with the cooperation and good will of others.

YOUR WORLD PSYCHOLOGY SECTION TWO
KEY POINTS

- We human beings, in anything we undertake, are always attempting to satisfy ourselves emotionally in some shape or form. It can be argued that everything we do is out of self-interest.
- When we have experienced phases of our lives that we remember as particularly happy it is probably also the case that our relationships at that time were working well
- All of us carry round our individual version of "the world according to us"' or our mental map
- If we want to develop high quality relationships with others it is important to willingly and respectfully step into "their worlds" as that is where they exist.
- High quality relationships benefit everyone as they enhance and improve the quality of our lives and experiences.
- Being genuinely interested in others and their lives is a healthy basis for creating solid relationships.

- We tend to gravitate towards other people who share our views, beliefs and values. While this is a secure and reassuring thing to do, it does have a limiting effect upon our lives by excluding others who are different to us.
- The biggest obstacle to the creation and nurturing of rewarding personal relationships is often the need we have to be right and have our ideas and attitudes prevail.

LEARNED THINKING

ACHIEVING SELF-KNOWLEDGE
AND SELF-CONTROL

"Did you ever imagine you could be so strong?
Watch your fear just turn into relief
And see your doubt become your own belief"

Beth Orton, "Pass In Time", Central Reservation

In the introductory chapter I asked you a very direct question:

"Why have you decided to read this book?"

Now I want to ask you another one:

"Has it lived up to the expectations of providing you with a fresh chance to bring about improvement in your life?"

I have no doubt that, as you have been reading, your mind will have been involved in a number of internal conversations. It is quite likely that you have at times found yourself agreeing with some parts; at others you may have found yourself questioning or even disputing some of what you have read. If you have been engaged in this way then you have been busy weighing up all the ideas and notions against the knowledge and beliefs that you already possess. As a result, you may already be able to assimilate these new concepts into your personal world view. On the other hand, you may still have questions that you would like to ask or ideas that you would like to test out.

Over the many years that I have been teaching the MindSpan principles to groups around the country, there have been several occasions on which the same reaction has been aired. The fact that this has arisen quite independently on each occasion makes it worthy of attention and response.

It has gone something like this:

"But isn't this all just about the importance of being an optimist? Wouldn't a person get the same results by simply being optimistic?"

While I have always recognised and acknowledged that this is a reasonable and worthwhile query, I am certain that the answer to this is simply "no". However, I have found that, in the context of a training event, supplying the full and detailed answer that I would really want to offer has not always been quite so straightforward.

So, I would really like to address this question here. It may be something that you have been thinking about yourself. If so, then it is even more important to deal with it now.

I want to explain carefully and clearly that, while raw optimism does, indeed, have its part to play, successfully applying the MindSpan approach requires a much more sophisticated and purposeful set of mental processes than doing what is little more than simply, and I would argue, quite passively, adopting a particular attitude or frame of mind.

In his enormously important book, *Learned Optimism*, Martin Seligman took popular and commonly-held ideas and turned them into a set of fresh and convincing arguments about the ways in which human beings can actively shape their approaches to life and, therefore, the quality of the lives they lead. In Seligman's view it was not enough to merely describe the states of optimism and pessimism and the influences on the individual these might have. For him the crucial point was to know what to do with this knowledge.

Seligman's achievements shake up and give newer and much more precise meanings and purposes to these received notions.

He starts his book by looking at the essential differences between optimistic and pessimistic perspectives on life. It is Seligman's belief that we all vary between these two ways of looking at life; in their extreme forms, both optimism and pessimism hold benefits and dangers. Optimists, for example, have proven health and career advantages, but these are tempered by the possibility that such individuals can also become self-delusional, with all its potentially damaging results. Pessimists, on the other hand, are much more prone to personal illness and unfulfilled ambition, but are fortunate at least in being very aware and realistic in their dealings with others, especially in business.

Furthermore, pessimists who exhibit their dominant trait regularly are also very likely to develop what Seligman describes as "learned helplessness", especially if their way of explaining their shortcomings, or what he calls their "explanatory style", convinces them that the way they experience and understand the world is a permanent state of affairs and there is nothing they can do to change this. By contrast, Seligman contends that those people who display only temporary pessimism, even if this manifests itself intermittently for years on end, can change their thinking and consequently the nature of their lives by learning new habits of thought – "learned optimism".

Seligman declares that if we take on this new understanding we are able to seize hold of and change our approach. Consequently, we are able to banish the old determinist belief that we are trapped within our natures, unable to change the way we are and the results that life will inevitably bring us. By making an active decision to take advantage of the choice that he has made explicit and available to us, we can all now learn to use a new flexibility in our thinking and the ways in which we respond to the difficulties that life throws at us.

I hope that this discussion is beginning to ring bells for you. On one level, Seligman's ideas are vital to countering the view that to deal with life all that is needed is optimism. On another, much more important level, you will also better understand how this relates to the essential purposes of this book. Like the tenets of "Learned Optimism", the MindSpan principles are straightforward but sophisticated. They are built upon the belief that if we can become fully aware of the effects and limits of our own thinking we can take considered steps to engage and apply a whole new set of cognitive skills. As

Seligman points out, a sense of helplessness about our lives can be learned, but it can also be unlearned; once this happens the possibilities of life are quite literally unlimited. MindSpan provides the vehicle and the tools by which transforming the fundamentals of the way we think can be successfully put into practice.

So let us consider the journey of this book. As you have read and worked your way through it, you have been offered the opportunity not just to be introduced to a large number of new ideas. You have also been invited to discover just how these principles and approaches can be set to work, if you choose to do so, in the everyday reality of your life. While we have been concerned with understanding the importance of our thinking, simply knowing that we think is not enough. We need to be able to think about our thinking and be willing and able to shape it to our own ends.

My intention has been to help you become aware of the self-limiting and self-defeating patterns of much of your thinking and self-beliefs. When this is successfully accomplished you can begin to learn, develop and thrive by developing more positive self-talk. This is not mere optimism, but the conscious application of a set of powerful skills and understandings that can bring growth and personal fulfilment. Instead of allowing the adversities of life to trigger off unconscious, destructive beliefs and explanations about ourselves, MindSpan, like "Learned Optimism", calls into action a set of techniques and mental activities that can bring about much better outcomes in a fully aware and conscious manner.

Like Seligman's book, MindSpan does not offer a panacea to all life's ills but it does provide a robust and resilient method through which a better future can be consciously and optimistically, constructed.

NEXT STEPS FOR YOU

*"A journey of a thousand miles
starts with a single step."*

Mao Tse Tung

If you have enjoyed this book, and developed an appetite to learn and do much more in your life then I am very pleased with this outcome and I trust that you are too. To paraphrase Chairman Mao's famous saying, you have set out on a new, exciting and rewarding journey.

By taking the opportunity to look deeply into yourself and examine how you think and act, you have developed a fresh and heightened level of self-awareness and enhanced personal potential.

Remember, and carry at the front of your mind, two central messages that we have uncovered and explored:

The first of these is that your thinking and your focus will always drive the results that you achieve.

The second message is that you can never outperform your own self-image. The better the way you see yourself, the more improved your personal results will be in all areas of your life.

To continue developing, it is essential that you carry on working, every day, on these two areas.

As you decide upon your next steps it is, again, vital that you create for yourself an understanding of what this means in terms of the real actions you can choose to make. What happens next rests entirely on your decisions, so it really is worth spending some time considering how you intend to progress from here. Start by recognising your achievement in getting to this point; by engaging in this book you have already come a very long way and as a result you now really do have at your disposal the potential to truly enhance your life from this day forward.

In summary, this book has provided you with many tangible tools:

- A personal performance audit
- An ongoing life audit
- A rigorous method of setting personal goals for yourself
- An ever-involving achievement log
- An appreciation log
- Your personal affirmations
- Access to the MindSpan website at www.mind-span.co.uk
- Commitment to new regular affirmations (self-talk) creates new neural pathways (beliefs) in the brain
- Visualising an activity or experience, which allows the sub-conscious and central nervous

system to respond as though it were really happening

- Regular positive affirming and visualisation of future performances and achievements which can strengthen inner belief and desire

These are very powerful resources to own and use. Use them well. Return to them every day and make them an integral part of your life.

Most importantly, I hope this book has provided you with a new path, new ways of thinking and new ways of being. Nurture these and they will serve you well for the rest of your life.

I wish you well as you go on to enjoy the benefits.

Gavin Drake

BIBLIOGRAPHY

Stop Thinking and Start Living, Richard Carlson, published by Thorsons

Man's Search For Meaning, Viktor E. Frankl, published by Rider

Psycho-Cybernetics 2000, Bobbe Sommer, published by Thorsons

The Road Less Travelled, M. Scott Peck, published by Rider

Goals!, Brian Tracy, published by Berrett-Koehler

Emotional Intelligence, Daniel Goleman, published by Bloomsbury

Being Happy, Andrew Matthews, published by Media Masters

Positive Thinking, Vera Peiffer, published by Element

What to say when you talk to Yourself, Shad Helmstetter, published by Thorsons

Authentic Happiness, Martin E. P. Seligman, published by Nicholas Brealey

Learned Optimism, Martin E. P. Seligman, published by Free Press

The Biology of Belief, Bruce H. Lipton, published by Hay House

Evolve Your Brain, Joe Dispenza, published by HCI Books

Getting Things Done, Allen, D. published by Piatkus

Choice, Collins, J. , published by Random House

Switch, Heath C. and Heath D. , published by Random House

Obliquity, Kay, J. , published by Profile

Drive, Pink, D. , published by Canongate

It's the thought counts, David R. Hamilton, published by Hay House

Happier, Tal Ben-Shahar, published by McGraw Hill

On my continuing journey of learning I have been inspired and positively impacted by the work of many great people. I am very grateful to these people and there are so many I'd like to mention that I'd probably need to print another book to include them all. However here are some of the most prevalent...

Sue, Ollie and Emily Drake

Jim Rohn

Deepak Chopra

Anthony Robbins

Dr Martin Seligman

Denis Waitley

Joe Dispenza

Dr Wayne Dyer

Bill Harris

Richard Jackson

Robert Cialdini

Eckhart Tolle

Daniel Goleman

Paul McVeigh

Steven Covey

Kath Temple

Sydney Banks

Steve Chandler

Nial Adams

Viktor Frankl

Mary Gober

Richard Carlson

James Allen

Napoleon Hill

Gavin Drake

THE AUTHORS

Gavin Drake has been working in the field of personal development and psychological performance for nearly two decades. He is founder of the organisation Inspire International Ltd and creator of the psychological performance programme, MindSpan. Through Inspire's seminars, training and coaching, Gavin has personally shared the MindSpan principles with many thousands of people in a number of European countries. His work has crossed many organisational and social boundaries including commercial organisations, government departments, education, prisons, the unemployed, charities and professional sport. Gavin's research into the varied fields of psychology continues as does his evolution of the MindSpan principles. He lives with his family in the countryside of Norfolk.

John Jackson has been involved in education and professional development for over 30 years. After a career in secondary education which led him into the field of teacher training he moved into the business sector as the Training and Development Manager of a large East Anglian retail company. Today his work is divided between teaching leadership and management courses for two university business schools, running his own consultancy, The People People, based in Norwich and membership of the MindSpan team. This is John's first book and follows a number of magazine articles on the subjects of learning theory and the management of education. He lives in Norfolk and has two adult daughters

Printed in Great Britain
by Amazon.co.uk, Ltd.,
Marston Gate.